OCT   1996

OCT   1996

THE ILLUSTRATED
MOTORCYCLE LEGENDS

HONDA

750F

ROY BACON

CHARTWELL
BOOKS, INC.

Previous page: The VFR 750F, 1994.

Acknowledgements

The author and publishers wish to acknowledge their debt to all who loaned material and photographs for this book. Most came from Honda material collected over the years, some gaps being filled from the author's own files. Other pictures which helped to complete the story came from *Motor Cycle News,* courtesy of the editor, and EMAP, whose archives hold the old *Motor Cycle Weekly* files. Thanks to all who helped.

Copyright © 1995 Sunburst Books

Published by
CHARTWELL BOOKS, INC.
A division of **BOOK SALES, INC.**
P.O. Box 7100
Edison, New Jersey 088 18-7100

ISBN 0 7858 0256 8

Designed by Anthony Cohen

Printed and bound in China

CONTENTS

EARLY DAYS

The man with the dream - Soichiro Honda.

Honda - the largest of them all, but the product of one man's dream which became his Honda Dream, on which he built an empire. Soichiro Honda, a technician who dominated grand prix racing, put the 'nicest people' on a Honda and his name came to mean 'motorcycle'. Truly, in the 1960s the two words were synonymous.

Born in 1906, the son of a blacksmith, Soichiro had a practical nature and by the 1930s had his own repair shop. He later went into making piston rings, found them tricky and learnt some technology. After the war he sold out and in October 1946 at Hamamatsu, he founded the Honda Tecnical Research Institute - a grand name for what was actually a small wooden shed, but it was to grow.

Honda loved vehicles, so it was natural that he should choose to produce a motorcycle, as the demand for cheap alternatives to trains and trams was enormous. Beginning with a batch of surplus army engines, he soon had machines up and running, albeit poorly, but they sold. Next came the first Honda engine, a 50cc two-stroke, which powered his model A, quickly followed by more, all of which were rather crude.

Already, Honda was looking ahead to produce a complete machine and late in 1949 the model D, the first Dream, was completed. It was still crude, with a 1930s European-style, pressed-steel frame to carry the 98cc engine, but it was good and successful. This gave Honda financial and sales problems, but he found Takeo

At the start there was the man, the shed and the model A.

Opposite: The step-through scooterette and this brilliant slogan brought the Honda name to the forefront.

Fujisawa who soon sorted that out and pointed Soichiro ahead to four-stroke engines.

The result was the overhead-valve model E of 146cc. Although not a very good machine, it was reliable, had good spares back-up and sold well. However, its cost was too high for true mass-market appeal, so Honda turned his mind to a clip-on engine. This led to the F model Cub, a 50cc two-stroke unit which could be fitted in minutes to a bicycle.

Production soared and the Cub soon accounted for 70% of all Japanese machine sales.

This success put Honda in the forefront of a home market battle that raged in Japan throughout the 1950s. The list of over one hundred makes rapidly diminished to eight, dropping to the present four in the next decade. It was a desperate time for Honda who invested heavily in new machine tools and fresh designs. For 1953 he produced the first Benly model, the J type which had good, modern looks. There was a brief exercise with a scooter, but this was overshadowed by a 250cc single built in 1955, the first Honda with an overhead camshaft.

The 50cc model F Cub clip-on was the first successful mass-market Honda, easy to fit to any bicycle in minutes.

The 1955 model SA, with a 246cc single-cylinder engine and, a first for Honda, an overhead camshaft. Leading-link forks and enclosed rear chain were features.

The first Benly was the model J of 1953 which had an 89cc engine, overhead valves, three speeds and suspension for both wheels.

SUPER CUB AND TWINS

As the 1950s came to an end, two important new models made their appearance, but a new problem arose. The models were the Super Cub and the first twin, the latter appearing in 1957 as the 247cc C70 with an overhead camshaft. This model was to be the basis for many varieties over the years.

The Super Cub was brilliant, fulfilling the 'Everyman' dream market worldwide. Inexpensive, but not cheaply built, it offered the right performance and created the step-thru scooterette using a 50cc four-stroke engine and scooter styling, but good-sized wheels to cope with dirt roads. Launched in 1958 and developed over the years but keeping its original looks, some 15 million had been sold by 1983, and it ran on to over 20 million by 1992 using 50, 70 and 90cc engines.

The problem was the saturation of the Japanese home market. Up until then, secure behind tariff walls, they had built for a docile public which was unable to buy anything other than Japanese machines. By the late 1950s this market had been exploited to the full and expansion abroad was needed to take the surplus. This required massive publicity, as the Japanese firms were unknown in Europe or the USA at that time.

In 1959 Japan built about three-quarters of a million machines and Honda ran a team in the 125cc TT in the Isle of Man, where they were seen as something of a joke, despite the expense of that one outing. Meanwhile, American Honda was launched, along with the famous slogan, 'You meet the nicest people on a Honda',

After the first C70 twin, this smaller, 125cc CB90 sports twin was introduced for 1958, setting a style which was used for some years.

and sales campaigns were initiated to target many new areas and outlets.

The single racing effort of 1959 was increased for 1960, the firm dominating the 125 and 250cc classes in 1961, and going on to be a major force in Grand Prix racing. The machines were based on a four-valve, twin-overhead camshaft engine concept using more and more cylinders. The outcome was a 50cc twin, 125cc four and five, 250cc four and six, 350 four and (297cc) six, and the powerful, but unwieldy 500cc four. In 1966 they won all five solo world makers titles but pulled out after 1967.

This activity brought immense publicity and enabled Honda to open offices in many countries to sell an ever-expanding range of singles and twins. The engine from the Super Cub was used to create sports models, expanded, took a trail format, became a miniature Monkey bike and led on to many forms of basic moped over the years. Some even reverted to a two-stroke engine, but the basic Soichiro promise of inexpensive but not cheap always held good.

The twins were introduced into Europe in 1961 by the C71, an ohc 250cc machine with electric start, plenty of pressings for the cycle parts and a good performance. It was soon joined by the sports CB71 which had much sharper styling and two

The sports 155cc CS95 from 1958 which retained the leading-link forks and square styling, but had upswept exhausts.

A very early Super Cub from 1959, the model type that gave the world two-wheeled transport - the 'Everyman' machine.

excellent 125cc twins, the touring C92 and sports CB92.

During this period Honda offered a range of production racing models following on the CR71, a modified stock machine, and a race kit for the 125cc twin. The racers appeared for 1962, four in number, all of which were sophisticated four strokes. The smallest was the 50cc CR110 with eight-speed gearbox, next came the 125cc twin CR93 and, fewer in number, the 250 and 305cc CR72 and CR77 twins. They were only built for three seasons, but the 125 in particular proved very popular.

A scooter, the Juno, with a 169cc flat-twin engine and a variable ratio hydraulic transmission system appeared around this time, but it was unsuccessful and was soon dropped. Otherwise, the twins ran on through the decade in more and more varieties.

While Honda was expanding, the European firms were contracting and concentrating on large-capacity models, mainly vertical twins. Their attitude was that Japan could build the mass-market, small machines and, in time, the customers would move on to their own larger models. Not the best strategy, for Honda UK adverts plugged the speed and competitive performance of their smaller twins which offered sophistication never seen elsewhere.

Before long the sales of the 50cc Honda, coded the C100 at first, had run to millions and were to continue for decade after decade.

Over 2,500,000 Nicest People Own a Fabulous HONDA 50

HONDA 50   C-100

The first European appearance of the racing Honda was at the 1959 TT where this 125 ran reliably but well off the pace.

The bubble burst in 1965 when Honda launched their CB450 twin, the Black Bomber. It offered twin overhead camshafts, torsion bar valve springs and 100mph performance. Maybe the handling was not that of a Norton, but customers weaned on small Hondas now progressed happily to the larger varieties.

The extent of the Honda range had grown to the point that in 1967 they listed no less than eight 125cc twins alone. That year saw the launch of another of their long runners, the CD175 twin. A simple commuter, it was to be a best seller for year after year, ranking second only to the Super Cubs. There were variations, as usual, for sports, for trail, for off-road, even a farming model, while the series format led Honda into the 1970s.

By 1961 the 125cc twin and this 250cc four dominated grand prix racing in their classes, winning both world titles.

The sports CS65 for 1965, typical of the use made of the step-thru engine to create other models.

The trail version of the step-thru, the 1967 CT90, which retained much of the stock machine, but added protection bars and a massive rear sprocket.

Below: The 50cc engine was also used for this CZ100 Monkey bike. This is a 1966 model.

Below right: The 1966 P25 was a basic moped, which had the engine built into the rear wheel. Known as the Little Honda, it was produced in Japan and Europe.

The first twin seen in Europe was the 247cc C71 Dream, along with the similar 305cc C76, both tourers featuring the Honda square style.

The sports versions of the twins were the CS71 and CS76, which had raised exhausts. This is a 1959 model.

The larger 155cc CA95 was another in the 1959 Honda Benly line, in this case fitted with pillion seat.

The sports CB92 in 1959 with its distinctive sharp-edged styling.

Above: The racing 125cc CR93 as listed for 1962-64, was a twin with four valves per cylinder, twin camshafts and five speeds.

The Juno scooter built as the 125cc M80 and 169cc M85, with a flat twin engine, sophisticated transmission and trailing-link forks.

This was the 125cc C92 Benly for 1961, still with the older styling.

Raised exhausts continued to distinguish the CS92 Benly in 1961.

By 1963 the CB72 had sharpened up with telescopic front forks, the CB77 following suit.

However, the C72 still kept the leading-link forks for 1965.

250 (C72)
£219 . 19 . 0d. Tax paid

While the CB72 ran on in its new form for 1965.

250 Super Sport (CB72)
£259 . 19 . 0d. Tax paid

Trail versions of the twins had both exhausts raised on the left. This is the 1966 CL77.

First in a long series of road twins which used much the same format was this 1967 SS125. Developed and enlarged, it was to sell in vast numbers.

In 1965 Honda launched the CB450 Black Bomber, their first large capacity road machine. With it came this CL450 trail version.

A stop further along the trial brought this SL350 of 1970 - still a twin, but a little better suited to the off-road life.

The CD175 was a best seller for many years. This is a 1973 model, but little altered from earlier versions.

CB750 AND EXPANSION

It was October 1968 when Honda unleashed their bombshell and once again moved the boundaries. The machine was the CB750 - four cylinders, overhead camshaft, five speeds, electric start, disc front brake - an unprecedented combination. Fours had existed from the earliest days of motorcycling, but always in small numbers. The new Honda differed, offering sophistication, full equipment, over 120mph, reliability, good electrics, a keen price and it was readily available. It sold and sold, and was to change the standards for ever.

Motorcycle sales picked up in the 1970s. Traffic congestion and massive rises in fuel prices encouraged this trend, so it became the smart way to travel in town. Honda were at the forefront of this drive, extolling the virtues of two wheels in all forms of the media, many far divorced from the traditional. One new line first seen in the USA was the All Terrain Cycle, or ATC, which used the 90cc engine of the step-thru to drive a three-wheel machine, with enormous, balloon tyres. These enabled it to run on any off-road surface, unimpeded by sand, mud, snow, grass or deep water. They were fun to ride and very practical on farm or in forest for carrying a man and his tools quickly to where they were needed.

The Honda range grew and grew, and included numerous small singles for commuting, road, trail, moto-cross, enduro, trials and even road racing. Most of the mid-range consisted of twins ranging from 125 to 450cc, and in 1974 this was extended to include the CB500T, whose lengthy camshaft chain was not to make it one of Honda's best products.

Earlier, in 1971, another four was added - the CB500 - while 1972 brought the CB350, both of which copied the lines of the CB750. In 1974 the smallest was stretched out to create the CB400F, a Honda classic which had all four exhaust pipes swept down to a single silencer on the right. With it came the CB550, a tourer, and a further ATC fitted with the 70cc engine.

October 1968 brought the first CB750, a sensation at the time with four cylinders, ohc, electric start, five speeds, disc brake and all readily available.

The first of the All Terrain Cycles was this 1970 US70, sold elsewhere as the ATC series and great fun to ride.

The sports SS50 of 1967, a popular model with teenagers.

The step-thru engine was also used in this ST50, also known as the DAX, and listed from 1969 in 50 and 70cc forms.

An alternative use for the engine was in this CF70 Chaly scooterette, which was listed for some years.

For trial use the single became the SL125 which worked well enough.

The single soon grew into the CB125S, later the CB125J, which used to get many people to work each day.

This CB100 was a commuter single with ohc, which performed well in traffic.

From the CL and SL series came the better-known XL. This 1976 XL250 shows the range style.

The larger XL350 as advertised in the USA for 1976.

SPECIFICATIONS ON THE ELSINORE™ CR-250M

Engine
  Type..Single-cylinder two-stroke.
  Bore and Stroke..70 mm x 64.4 mm.
  Displacement...........248 cc.
Transmission..5-speed close-ratio.
Suspension
  Front..long-travel telescopic fork.
  Rear..Swing arm with long-travel refillable shock absorbers.

Brakes....Internal expanding shoe.
Clutch.....Wet disc multi-plate.
Tire Size
  Front...3.00 x 21.
  Rear....4.00 x 18.
Frame..Semi-double cradle.

Ignition system..Flywheel Magneto.
Dimensions and Capacities
  Length................84.3 in.
  Width..................35.0 in.
  Height.................44.9 in.
  Wheelbase............57.1 in.
  Fuel Capacity........1.8 gal.
  Dry Weight...........214 lbs.

The Elsinore range was listed for moto-cross, this being the 1973 CR250M.

At the other end of the scale there was the Mini Trail Z50, models like this being raced in Japan.

Below: An ohc single engine was used for the XR75 moto-cross model, an alternative to the more usual two-strokes.

The ohc single engine was used for the trials TL125S model, which proved to be a popular first motorcycle for many.

Equipped with twin carburettors, the CB200 joined the CD175 as the sports machine.

This 1976 CB350 shared many common parts with the CB250, both middle-weight twins offering a useful performance.

The largest twin for the '70s was the CB500T, developed from the CB450 and noted for the length of its cam chain.

In 1971 the CB500-four appeared, similar to the 750, but with its own style of silencers.

The CB400F was developed from the CB350, which was based on the CB500. It became a Honda classic.

GOLD WING AND CBX SIX

Late in 1974 Honda launched a new four at the Cologne show - using a totally different layout to create a tourer to challenge Harley-Davidson and BMW in their home markets. For this they used a 1000cc watercooled, flat-four engine with belt-driven, single overhead camshafts and complex construction. It drove a five-speed gearbox and thence by shaft to the rear wheel which had a disc brake, as did the front.

Catalogued as the GL1000, the new tourer was listed as the Gold Wing and its comprehensive specification brought its dry weight up to 580lb. Scorned as the Lead Wing, it soon showed that with the mass low down it cornered better than expected, and thousands found it ideal for its job. Quiet, without vibration, fast, reliable, not too thirsty and able to carry all the weight people added to it.

For 1975 two sports fours, the CB750F and CB550F were added, followed the next year by another long runner, the simple and basic ohv CG125, a model still in the lists some two decades later. During 1976 Honda introduced the CB750A, which had a two-speed automatic transmission. Around this point Honda returned to racing, running large-capacity fours in endurance events to dominate the major races from 1976 to 1980. They introduced a Honda 125 race series to the UK in 1977 which ran for four seasons.

Late in 1974 Honda launched the Gold Wing, a massive and complex machine, which proved to be an ideal tourer.

As the 1970s drew to a close, Honda brought in a whole new series of models, although they did retain some of the favourites, such as the C50, C70 and C90 step-thrus, the ATC, the CG125, the off-road XL series, and the mopeds on which so many took their first Honda ride.

There were major changes in 1978, the most exciting being the fabulous six-cylinder CBX, whose 1047cc engine featured twin overhead camshafts, four valves per cylinder and all the expected Honda style. The range was also enhanced by the addition of the CX500, a machine which had a watercooled V-twin engine, four-valve heads, but pushrod actuation from a single, central camshaft. The engine was set across the frame to suit shaft final drive and, after some early problems, the model settled down to a successful run, proving popular with despatch riders.

From 1979 onwards the CBX and the Gold Wing were both built in a plant in Ohio, USA, close to so many of the Wing's best customers. There were Honda factories in Europe, Africa, Central and South America, as well as in Asia and their Japanese homeland.

Several new twins, sold as Dreams in Europe and Hawks in the USA, were introduced for 1978, the largest of which was the CB400T, which featured a three-valve head, balance shafts and Honda convention. The CB250T was its twin, except for engine size, so suffered from the weight it had to tow along. There was also a CB400 automatic with a two-speed gearbox, the basic CD185T for the commuter, the CB125T, which could run through the red zone of the rev-counter to 13,000rpm, and the NF75 step-thru scooter.

Two sports fours were introduced in 1975. This CB750F was the larger and copied the style of the CB400F.

The smaller of the sports models was this CB550F, which took the style of the CB750F and offered a good performance.

The basic commuter model which ran for two decades was the ohv CG125, simple and reliable.

Above: The MT125 in water-cooled form, which was used for the successful Honda race series.

Right: The C50 step-thru as in 1977. It was hardly altered at all subsequently, and yet continued to sell well for many years.

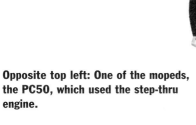

Opposite top left: One of the mopeds, the PC50, which used the step-thru engine.

Opposite top right: The Camino, or PA50, which relied on two-stroke power and had automatic transmission.

Opposite below: PF50 models came in two forms, both with a single-speed transmission. This is the Amigo, which used the two-stroke engine.

The Novio PF50 model had the four-stroke engine from the step-thru and modified style.

The mighty CBX was introduced for 1978, with six cylinders, twin camshafts, 24 valves and a style reminiscent of the racing Honda sixes of the '60s.

Above: Loved and loathed, the V-twin CX500 which had some early troubles but became one of Honda's best.

Just the thought, thought and design has been extended to the frame and other components which result in good handling, roadholding and braking characteristics but still retaining a lightweight feel. Many components have been located closer to the centre of gravity than with other traditional machines, resulting in a centralising of the machine mass; there is high ground clearance, new Honda rear suspension dampers (FVQ), special tread, low profile tyres and Honda's unique low maintenance Comstar wheels.

COMSTAR WHEELS. For years, Honda has been involved in basic wheel research, developing a new wheel design that would combine optimum strength, unsprung weight and ride characteristics. The problem has been mating the superior strength of cast wheels with the smooth-riding flex of conventional wire spoke wheels. The result is the Honda Comstar Wheel, it's different from anything you've ever seen before. The angled spoke plates are made of steel for strength and flexibility. The hollow body rim is aluminium alloy for extraordinarily lightweight, strength and beauty.

The entire configuration of the wheel provides a combination of incredible strength and low unsprung weight with up-to-the-minute good looks. In typical Honda fashion, the Comstar wheel has been thoroughly race proven on the Honda factory RCB Racing machine. These Comstar equipped machines, incidentally, captured the 1976 European Endurance Championship.

The two-speed automatic CB400A retained the podgy style of the series, the others soon changed.

The basic commuting twin for 1978 was the CD185T Benly, which retained a single overhead camshaft.

Sports alternative for 1978 was this CB125T which would rev through its red band.

A scooter step-thru for 1978 was the NF75 which used a two-stroke engine driving automatic transmission.

TWIN CAMS AND THE NR

The move to twin overhead camshafts and four-valve heads went further in 1979, when the sports CB900F and touring CB750K replaced the older CB750, which stayed on in limited edition form for a year. The CB650 retained the earlier engine form, while the CB400N and CB250N replaced the T models and had a much leaner style. The 50cc Honda Express was added at the other end of the range; very basic, it sold well. For the commuter, the earlier twin was stretched to become the CD200T and an ATC110 was added. The CB50J offered the learner a small Honda with large-machine style, and a trio of XR enduro models from 80 to 500cc joined the XL trail series, all with four-stroke engines, unlike the CR moto-cross machines. Promotion of the off-road range was aided by Honda winning the 500cc world moto-cross title, a feat they would repeat seven times during the '80s.

In road racing they continued to be successful in endurance events and at the TT, but their return to the Grand Prix circuit failed. Determined to stick to a four-stroke but restricted to four cylinders, they produced the NR500 (New Racer) which had eight valves for each stretched-out, oval cylinder. Along with this radical layout, they used a monocoque chassis which gave limited access to the engine and 16 inch wheels, unlike the rest of the field. The first race was a disaster, both machines retiring, and two years' hard work failed to make it a real contender, so it was dropped but not forgotten.

Twin-cam, four-valve heads went onto the fours in 1979 to produce the fine sports CB900F.

The hottest of the road models introduced for 1980 was the CB1100R, a replica of the endurance machines. The CBX was fitted with the Honda Pro-link rear suspension, a rising-rate system developed on the works moto-cross racers, while the Gold Wing was stretched out to 1085cc and given air-assisted suspension, front and rear, to become the GL1100. A custom CB900C was introduced for the USA.

The CB750K Classic was offered for one year only, the stock model plus a cockpit fairing, but lower down the scale more significant machines appeared. One was the CB250RS, an excellent single-cylinder model which used a four-valve engine. The CD200T was joined by the custom styled CM200T, while some two-strokes were added in the form of the H100, the sports MB50 moped and its matching MT50 trail brother. Off-road there was the XR200 enduro single, the moto-cross CR80R and the Z50R, a monkey bike in moto-cross style.

More luxury was added to the Gold Wing for 1981 to produce the De Luxe version which came with a fairing as standard, and a top box and panniers offered as options which nearly all buyers added. The CB900F2 complete with fairing joined the basic model. A CB750F sports model was included alongside the tourer, but it was a new version of the CX500 which featured the major change.

The touring four became the twin-cam, four-valve CB750K in 1979 to continue the work begun a decade earlier.

The old four was offered as the Limited Edition CB750SS for just one year, complete with fairing.

The 1979 CB650 four used a single-camshaft engine in the older form.

In a few short months the sports twins were revamped to present a leaner line which proved popular. This is the CB400N Super Dream.

Very basic, very easy to use and consequently a good seller, the Honda Express NC50 used a two-stroke engine and automatic transmission.

The ATC110 joined the ranks of three wheelers for work, being fun to ride.

For 1979 the basic commuter became the CD200T, its single cam and four speeds proving to be ideal for the daily grind to work.

Above: Learner CB50J model which copied
the style of the larger singles and twins.

The largest of the enduro machines was the XR500, which was new for
1980, fitted with a four-valve engine.

Trial XL125S for 1978. The series was also built in 100, 185, 250 and 500cc models.

The CB1100R was new for 1980. It was derived from the successful works machines, and had many special parts.

The 1978 moto-cross CR250S Red Rocket model which was powered by a two-stroke single engine. The 125cc model was called the Red Bullet.

The early NR500 with monocoque frame and side radiators, standing in front of the later version, which was much modified. This was not a success, but the technology was used a decade later on the road.

The **CB250RS** proved to be a popular model following its introduction in 1980, as it was fast and handled well.

Custom style produced the 1980 CM200T from the basic CD road model.

Above: Honda offered a two-stroke motor-cycle in the form of the H100 single for 1980, another long runner in a popular class.

Left: 1980 brought a new pair of sports mopeds for the learner market, this the road MB50.

Above: The MT50 was the trail version of the sports mopeds introduced for 1980.

For Junior moto-cross there was the CR80R in 1980, a model in the mould of the larger machines.

Above left: Moto-cross, monkey style was the province of the Z50R of 1980.

Above right: The CB900F2 was created by adding a fairing to the stock model.

De Luxe version of the GL1100 which came well equipped for fast, easy travel.

Sports CB750F of 1981 which offered a fine performance from its four cylinders.

TURBO, CUSTOMS AND VEES

The technical news for 1981 was the addition of a turbocharger to the CX500 which came at a time when the turbo was making its way into the automotive scene. Honda chose to demonstrate their expertise by adding theirs to a small twin rather than a larger four - a much tougher task. They succeeded, but the result was complex, expensive, suffered from turbo-lag, and was no quicker than many existing fours. At the same time they offered a custom model CX500C which had suitable styling changes.

Maintaining the custom trend, they added the CM250T, which used the CB250N engine, while the Melody and Caren scooters were added to their moped list, plus the off-road PX50. Also off-road was the ATC185S using the XL-series engine, and the full-blooded CR450R moto-cross racer.

A host of new models was added for 1982, a year when Honda turned to the V-engine configuration in place of the in-line four. Not that they ignored this, adding the CB750F2 with fairing, the custom CB650SC, and the CBX550F and F2 (plain or faired), the latter with their disc brakes concealed so well that front wheel removal became a major task.

The new trend was highlighted by the VF750S, or V45 Sabre, and the custom style VF750C, or V45 Magna. Both used a watercooled, 90-degree, V-four engine with four valves per cylinder, six-speed gearbox, shaft final drive and an inadequate chassis which had Pro-link for the Sabre and twin shocks for the Magna. The machine which

The CX500 Turbo was a technically difficult, complex way of achieving no more than the CB900 could offer, but very clever.

retained the V-twin engine was the GL500 Silver Wing, a CX500 with a fairing in Gold Wing style fitted as standard.

Two small twins were added as the commuter CD125T and its custom brother, the CM125C, while the moped end of the range expanded with more variations of the Camino, Caren, Express and Melody models, the NH80 Lead scooter, and the Stream. The latter was a scooter-style machine with two rear wheels and a centre hinge to allow the main body, plus seat and rider, to bank left or right while the rear end, complete with 50cc engine and wheels, remained upright.

Off-road, the XL-series had revised Pro-link rear suspension, the largest moto-cross model became the CR480R and the ATC250R joined the others having three balloon tyres. From the XL-series came the FT500, a road model using the single cylinder, single camshaft, four-valve engine, and called Ascot in the USA after that famous circuit from whence its flat-track style came.

The same US origins brought the CL250S, more a road model than off-road, but having an extra low-speed or crawler ratio to augment its five-speed gearbox. Rather similar was the CT125, sold as a farm bike so fitted with a rack, protection bars and a prop stand on each side, but based on the well-established 125cc engine.

A custom CX500C version of the V-twin.

Based on the existing twin, the 1981 CM250T used custom styling along with the well-known engine.

CAREN DELUXE MOPED

Caren NX50 moped scooter of 1981, one of the many.

MOPED

The PX50 offered an automatic moped with trail machine tyres which worked well on or off road.

For commuting, the NS50 Melody scooter was offered in standard and de luxe forms, as automatic as it could be.

Above: For top level moto-cross there was the CR450R, not a machine for the novice.

Left: Another of the three-wheeled models was the ATC110S in the same form as the others, and just as much fun.

The 1982 CB750F2 had a fairing, but retained the in-line four engine concept.

This is the later CB650 from which the CB650SC Nighthawk was derived by fitting raised bars, a styled seat and four megaphone silencers.

By adding a fairing, the GL500 Silver Wing was created from the base CX500.

Concealed, and inaccessible, front disc brakes with anti-dive were to be a feature of the CBX550F model, also listed in faired F2 form.

The first of the V-four models was the VF750S, sold in the USA as the V45, and also built in custom form.

One of a pair of new, small twins for 1982 was the CD125T, a simple commuter.

In custom form the small twin became the CM125C with five speeds and styled to suit.

For 1982 the Camino was available in standard, sports and this special form.

Caren scooter in its 1982 form, fully automatic for easy riding.

The Express de luxe which was fitted with an engine shield, shopping basket and turn signals.

Introduced for 1982, this is the 1988 version of the
NH80 Lead, later called the Vision.

A strange scooter with three wheels and a centre hinge to allow the
front section to bank to left or right - the 1982 NV50 Stream. Odd
to ride but it worked.

Above: The ATC250R had a high-output engine, five speeds, good forks and Pro-link rear suspension, so went well.

Listed as Ascot in the USA and FT500 for Europe, this model used the single-cylinder engine, evoking machines of the past.

The CL250S was more a road than trail model, but had a crawler ratio in its gearbox to deal with off-road moments.

Sold as a farm bike, the CT125 used the well-established camshaft engine and had trail bike features to suit its purpose.

RACING AGAIN

Honda changed tack on the Grand Prix circuits for 1982, moving from the complex NR500 to the simple, three-cylinder, reed-valve, two-stroke NS500. In 1983 it gave Honda their first 500cc riders title, and for 1984 became the NSR500 V-four to win in 1985, 1987 and 1989.

The road model line-up for 1983 saw further consolidation of the V-engine type, the 750cc engine being fitted to a much improved chassis to give the VF750F. This line was extended by adding the VF400F in the same vein as a 90-degree, V-four engine with four valves per cylinder, water cooling and a super-sports specification.

Smaller than this, but similar, was the VT250F, a V-twin with the same format, while the VT500E went along a different route. It had a 52-degree V-angle and an off-set dual crankpin to reduce vibration. It retained the water cooling, although styled as if for air, and had an overhead camshaft to open the three valves of each cylinder. Thus it was not simply a CX500 with the engine turned, but did have shaft drive. In the USA it became the VT500C Shadow custom model and was joined by a larger VT750C and, for 1985, a VT1100C in the same style.

The transverse-vee twins grew up to become the CX650E and CX650T-turbo models, the latter much improved by the extra capacity, but still a complex way of merely matching the CB900. At the top end of the scale the Gold Wing Aspencade joined the stock model, fitted out with all manner of extras and named after the major US rally.

For 1983 the V-four engine was presented in a new frame, creating the VF750F, which was to be a successful model.

VF400F

The VF400F V-four with anti-dive and enclosed front discs joined the larger model.

VT250F

The VT250F V-twin was smaller, with only two cylinders, and was very similar to the 400.

VT500E
Euro Sport

For the VT500E the V-angle was narrowed, the style appeared as air cooled although it was not, and it kept the enclosed front brake.

CX650E
Euro Sport

In 1983 the transverse V-twin grew up to become the CX650E while retaining the features of the older model.

The turbo version was also enlarged to be the CX650TC but remained a complex solution to a simple problem.

Taking its name from the massive American rally, the GL1100A Aspencade was the grand tourer with it all.

SMART SMALL FRY

At the bottom end of the 1983 market the sports mopeds were revised to become the road MBX50S and trail MTX50S, joined by the MBX80F, which had a little more capacity. The Lead 125 scooter joined the smaller version, the CH125 Spacy scooter with its more futuristic styling was added, and the QR50 appeared for the junior moto-cross rider. More enduro and ATC models were introduced, some more serious than others, as well as a couple of trials models and a new, basic learner model, the ohc CB125RS.

There was no let-up from the world's largest motorcycle firm for 1984, the Gold Wing stretching out to become the GL1200 in both de luxe and Aspencade forms. The V-engine range also stretched to offer the VF1000F, much the same as the 750, and the VF1000R, which featured gear drive to its overhead camshafts and super looks as a limited edition package. The V-four VF500F2 completed the series in the same style as the 750 and was listed in the USA as the road Interceptor or custom Magna. The US market also had a VF1100C Magna in 1983 and the road model VF1100 Sabre the next year.

Convention produced the CBX750F, a transverse four which took the line a stage further, while the 250 single became the CBX250RS, which had twin overhead camshafts, and a radial four-valve head on the well-known model. In the USA tariffs reduced the fours' capacity to 696cc, resulting in the CB700SC Nighthawk, while the V-fours reduced to the VF700C and VF700F. Off-road, the largest trail model became the XL600R, the Melody model was revised, an ATC125M was added and the

The new version of the sports moped for 1983 was the MBX50S.

MBX125F joined its 80cc brother to offer racing style on the street. Yet another scooter moped, the SH50 City Express, was added to the many.

For 1985 the VF1000F2 Bol d'Or, which had a full fairing, joined the V-range, and three very diverse models were added. One was the XBR500, which used a four-valve, single-cylinder engine and was constructed in a style that was reminiscent of the past. The NS400R was bang up-to-date, for it had a V-three, two-stroke engine and all the style and looks of the works machines. There was also an NS250R parallel twin, and, later, an NSR250R V-twin, both expensive, fast, and seldom seen outside Japan. The third of the new stream was the CH250 Spacy scooter, which used a single-cylinder, overhead-camshaft, water-cooled engine, fully-automatic transmission, belt final drive and a laid back style.

Most of the other models new to the range were off-road, headed by a whole series of moto-cross machines which ranged from the Cadet class CR50R to the serious CR500R, based on the works model that was to win the world title for five years from 1985 and again in 1992. There was also a Paris-Dakar version of the XL600LM, the TLM50 and TLR250 trials models and the XR250R and XR600R enduro machines. Plus the trail MT50S and MTX125R.

There had been early problems with the V-four engines and Honda made a tremendous effort to redeem their reputation, the result being the VFR750F of 1986. It was lighter, used an aluminium frame, had more power, the gear drive to the camshafts, and succeeded to become a great motorcycle. It was backed by the race-styled NS125F at the bottom end of the range and the CB350S, a twin-cylinder machine which had three valves per cylinder and air cooling, and was designed for economy and minimal maintenance.

With learner riders restricted to 125cc and reduced power, Honda offered this MTX125R to give them the off-road style they sought.

This 1983 road model MBX80F came with a belly pan and offered a little more capacity to buyers.

The Lead NH125 scooter followed came the lines of the smaller model, but gave more performance.

Above: Styling was the special feature of the Spacy CH125 scooter which used a water-cooled, ohc single engine and automatic transmission.

The QR50 was for the Junior moto-cross rider, using a two-stroke engine and automatic transmission.

This ATC200E had a dual-range transmission and came with front and rear carriers plus a trailer hitch for off-road working.

A basic learner model for 1983, the CB125RS based on the larger single and using the simple ohc engine.

In 1984 the Aspencade was stretched further to become the GL1200A, fitted with more equipment than ever.

New for 1984 was the larger VF1000F V-four in super-sports trim.

The VF1000R was a limited edition model with gear drive to its camshafts and many road race features.

A smaller V-four was the VF500F2 which copied the production racing style of the 1000.

The CBX750F was more conventional with its in-line engine, but it kept the cockpit fairing and belly pan.

A radial four-valve head and twin camshafts were features of the CBX250RS twin of 1984.

Above: For 1984 the trail single was stretched out to become the XL600R. A year later this XL600LM Paris-Dakar version was added.

Race style for the learner was one feature of the MBX125F of 1984.

New for 1984, the SH50 City
Express scooter.

Below: With fairing, the V-four
became the VF1000F2 Bol d'Or for
1985.

New Model for 1985

New Model for 1985

With its radial, four-valve engine, the 1985 XBR500 single was another attempt to recapture the past.

Based on the racing triple's concept, the NS400R had a three-cylinder, two-stroke engine using high technology.

The laid back scooter for 1985 was the CH250 Spacy, which used a four-stroke single engine and automatic transmission.

The CR250R moto-cross model was very similar to the top class 500.

XL600LM

Above: The Paris-Dakar version of the XL600LM trail single was introduced for 1985, with a 28-litre capacity fuel tank.

One of the 1985 trials models was this TLR250 which used the four-stroke single engine.

Enduro riders could choose between the XR250R and XR600R singles, both of which had twin carburettors. This is the larger.

The MT50S sports moped was introduced in 1985.

Left: The larger MTX125R seen here was also available as a 200 with a similar specification.

Below: Gear-drive to the camshafts, light-alloy frame, Pro-link rear suspension and anti-dive front end were a few features of the 1986 VFR750F, a fine machine.

The NS125F matched the race style, but was power restricted for the learner market.

Below: The CB350S twin used an old engine concept in a new frame to produce a basic, mid-range model.

BACK TO IN-LINE FOURS

By 1987 Honda had realised that their V-engined range was not succeeding, due to a combination of high price, early problems and no perceived advantages, so they looked back at their roots and came up with the CBR600F and CBR1000F, both of which used transverse-four engines with water cooling, four valves per cylinder and chain drive to the twin overhead camshafts. To this they added bodywork which enclosed all the mechanics and allowed the machine to slip easily through the air. The result was a success, both machines offering the right performance at the right price.

Despite the new in-line fours, Honda still kept going on the V-front, introducing the 600V Transalp. This took the VT500E engine, enlarged it, and fitted it to a trail-type chassis with a 21 inch front wheel and a fairing to produce a machine that worked well enough on the road and could venture a little way off it. The XL-series single was enlarged to produce the NX650 Dominator, less off-road, thanks to a small fairing. It worked well and made a successful big thumper. A year later the NX125 joined it in matching style. On the competition front, Honda built a limited number of 125 and 250cc racing machines, and trail and moto-cross models continued to be listed.

One of Honda's great models was introduced in 1988 - the VFR750R, a racing machine that was street legal but no race replica. Coded as the RC30 and Honda 15, it was developed from the highly successful factory RVF750, copying its style, finish, single-side swinging arm, aluminium frame and wonderful V-four engine, which had titanium connecting rods and a camshaft gear train drive further developed to reduce noise and backlash. Out of town the RC30 was superb, on the race track it proved a winner.

For 1987 Honda introduced full enclosure of the mechanics using slippery plastic for two models, one of which was this CBR600F four.

The larger V-twin engine was used for another new 1988 model, the NTV600 Revere which slotted it into a twin-beam frame with shaft drive in a single-sided swinging arm. Aimed at the mature rider, its emphasis was on the engine's easy manner, while in the USA it became the chain-drive NT650 Hawk, and was joined by the VT800C Shadow custom which retained the shaft drive.

For 1989 the accent was on improvements, but the CB450S, a mid-range twin, and the NS125R with full fairing were added. The CB450S was a throw-back to the earlier three-valve engines and had been listed in the USA since 1982 in road and custom forms. The Vision Met-in scooter moped with revised styling and more storage space was also introduced, as well as another enduro model, the XR80R. In the USA the PC800 Pacific Coast V-twin model was produced to sell leisure riding by hiding all the mechanics under extensive panelling, but although a good machine, it was not a success. The USA was also offered the GB500, built on the lines of the XBR500.

Rally touring was the province of the Transalp 600V which used the narrow-angle V-engine and had some off-road fittings.

The larger 1987 transverse four was the CBR1000F which differed from the CBR600F in ignition, tank size, suspension and brakes as well as capacity.

The NX650 Dominator which used the XL-series single engine for its dual duties on and off the road, this a 1992 model.

For road racing Honda built a limited number of 125 and 250 machines, this the RS250R of 1991.

The RC30 was a street-legal racing machine that incorporated much of Honda's advanced technology. It was very successful.

Above: Named the Revere, the NVT600 used the narrow-angle, V-twin engine to create a tourer for the mature rider but it failed to sell.

Using an old-style engine, the CB450S was another mid-range model built for some years.

The NS125R was offered for 1989 complete with full fairing, a learner model with full race style.

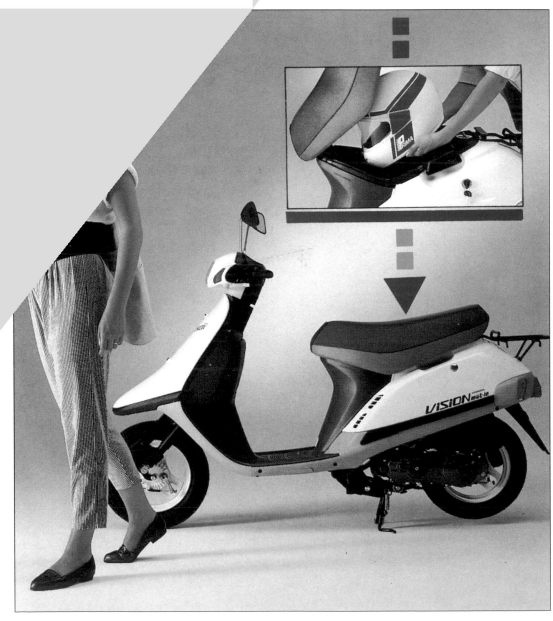

STRETCHED WINGS AND OTHERS

n 1990 Honda turned their attention to the touring market. The Gold Wing retrieved lost performance by stretching to a flat-six engine and more capacity to become the GL1500. Massive, but ultra-smooth, it continued to carry all that was asked of it. To back up the Wing, Honda added the ST1100 Pan European, which had its watercooled, V-four engine axis along the frame, so that each pair of four-valve heads could be seen inside the extensive fairing. Shaft drive followed naturally to produce an impressive sports-tourer well able to cover distance at speed.

The super-sports range was expanded to include the VFR400R, coded the NC30, a product of the Japanese home market class. It followed the style of the RC30 and its race-bred technology of gear-driven camshafts, special parts and a 13,000rpm engine speed. In total contrast was the CN250 scooter which used the ohc single engine and automatic transmission in a machine offering radical styling and a feet-forward riding stance. It had been in the US line as the Helix since 1986.

A 10th Anniversary, limited edition GL1500SE was listed for 1991, when the CBR600F had an extensive redesign, and the Transalp was joined by the even larger XRV650 Africa twin. This was a replica of the factory NXR which had won the Paris-Dakar rally four times and was followed by the larger XRV750. Both of these machines had a fairing and massive fuel tank. At the other end of the scale came the EZ90M Cub, an off-road fun model with two-stroke engine, automatic transmission and futuristic styling.

The new decade brought the GL1500 for 1990, with a flat-six engine and even more equipment than before.

The ST1100 with an in-line, V-four engine was introduced in 1990 in Europe for touring.

The RC30 gained a smaller brother for 1990, the VFR400R, or NC30, which copied the style of the RC30 and ran its engine at a very high speed.

Really laid back seating was the theme of the CN250 of 1990. It had ample storage space, a four-stroke single engine and automatic transmission.

Below: The CBR600F was extensively redesigned for 1991 to maintain its position at the front of its class.

Above: For 1992 the XRV750 Africa Twin was listed, based on the Transalp and smaller XRV650, all narrow-angle V-twins.

By way of contrast there was the EZ90M, an automatic off-road model that featured electric start.

NR750, FIREBLADE, RETRO

I n 1991 the revolutionary NR750 made its debut. Based on the technology of the 1979 factory NR500, it had been developed from a mock-up displayed in Tokyo in 1980. As with the racer, it had a V-four engine, eight valves per oval cylinder, and each piston supported on twin connecting rods. The machine incorporated all the sophistication that was Honda engineering and was extremely expensive, with production scheduled for around 700 to 1000 units.

The hot model for 1992 was the CB900RR FireBlade, a hyper-sports in-line four destined to be a top seller, while anti-lock brakes became an option for the ST1100. The VT600C Shadow, a custom model first seen in the USA in 1988, used the V-twin engine in a hard-tail style and different mood. From the past came the CB750 four, air-cooled but with four-valve heads, and two smaller ohc twins, the basic CB250 and more basic CD250U, both of which were air-cooled with a simple specification. The hot learner single became available without the fairing as the NSR125F.

It was consolidation for 1993, when the CB1000 retro model and enlarged NTV650 Revere were added, and revisions for 1994. That year saw the RC45 replace the RC30 and Honda stepped up their attack on the race track, using a new 750cc V-four engine which embodied much of their most advanced technology. A race kit to boost the considerable stock power, a new twin-spar aluminium frame, special forks and massive disc brakes all indicated the firm's determination to produce a winner.

At the same time the VFR750F lost some weight and gained some NR750 style, the

Sophisticated and exclusive, the NR750 was the most advanced Honda yet, sporting the most sophisticated technology from its eight-valve engine to its 15,000 rpm rev limit and titanium-tinted windscreen.

Transalp had a face lift and the FireBlade was further improved. Honda introduced the CB500, a twin which followed the lines of the CB1000, using a modern engine in a retro-style frame to offer a light and versatile model for Europe. After a seven-year absence, the XR600R enduro model returned to offer up-to-date, off-road capabilities.

It was business as usual for 1995, with minor changes and revisions to colours and graphics for most models. The one newcomer was the CA125 Rebel, a custom-style machine previously sold only in Japan and fitted with the well-proven, twin-cylinder, single-camshaft engine. One model which was thoroughly revised was the highly successful CBR600F, which gained an all-new engine, modified forks and new front discs, along with a solenoid-controlled air-intake duct system.

So the mighty Honda empire rolled on, producing many other products in addition to their motorcycles. As always, there were variants for different countries, models for the Japanese home market and more machines than anyone else.

Nearly half a century on from the small hut - the dream had come a very long way.

The CB900RR FireBlade appeared in 1992 and immediately became a best seller, dominating its class.

Custom style was offered by the VT600C Shadow with its hard-tail looks and V-twin engine.

Harking back to 1968 for the retro scene brought the CB750 in 1992, as before but updated in many ways.

Another model reminiscent of the past was this air-cooled CB250 twin, which was very similar to the Benly of earlier years.

Above: In 1993 this CB1000 four combined some past features with a modern, 16-valve, water-cooled engine.

Above right: Even more basic was the CD250U, simplicity for the commuter, but it was not to catch on.

Right: Hundreds of changes were made to the VFR750F for 1994 to revitalise a popular model.

Below: The fabulous RC45 which replaced the highly successful RC30 in 1994 to offer the best of Honda's advanced technology.

Above: The Revere stretched out to become the NTV650 in 1993.

The Transalp as offered for 1994.

In 1993 Honda still offered small scooters, such as this SJ50 Bali.

A reminder of where it all started, the step-thru scooterette. This is a 1980 C50.

HONDA NAMES

These can be used for more than one machine type but the following generally applies. Some are USA only, others Europe only; the USA tended to have more names than elsewhere. The model code is included along with the machine type.

Aero - scooter - NB, NH
Africa Twin - enduro - XRV
All Terrain Cycle - ATC
Amigo - moped - PF
Ascot - custom flat track - FT, VT
Aspencade - Gold Wing - GL

Bali - moped scooter - SJ
Benly Super Sport - CB
Benly Touring - CA, CD
Big Red - ATC

Camino - moped - PA
Caren - scooter step-thru - NX
Chaly - scooter step-thru - CF
City Express - moped scooter - SH
Cub - rear wheel engine - F
Cub - trail monkey - EZ
Cub - step-thru - C
Custom - CB, CM, CX

Dax - midi - ST
Dominator - trail - NX
Dream - D
Dream Sport - CE, CS

Dream Touring - C, CA

Elite - scooter - CH, SA, SB, SE
Elsinore - moto-cross - CR, MR, MT
Express - moped - NA, NC
Express - scooter - NX

Fat Cat - enduro - TR
Fireblade - super sports - CBR
Fourtrax - four wheels - TRX
Fourtrax Foreman - four wheel drive - TRX

Gold Wing - tourer - GL
Graduate - moped - PF
Gyro - scooter - NN, TG

Hawk - sports - CB, NT
Helix - scooter - CN
Hondamatic - automatic - CB, CM
Hurricane - super sports - CBR

Interceptor - road sports - VF, VFR, VT, VTR
Interstate - GL

Juno - scooter - K

Lead - scooter - NH
Little Honda - moped - P, PC

Magna - custom - VF
Melody - moped scooter - NB, ND, NP, NS, NT
Met-in - Vision scooter - SA
Mini-Trail - monkey bike - Z
Motosport - trail - SL, XL

Nighthawk - semi-custom - CB
Novio - moped - PF, PM

Odyssey - four wheels - FL

Pacific Coast - tourer - PC
Pan European - tourer - ST
Passport - step-thru - C
Port-Cub - step-thru - C

Rebel - custom - CMX
Red Rocket - motocross - CR
Reflex - trials - TLR
Revere - tourer - NTV

Runaway - moped - NU

Sabre - sports - VF
Scrambler - CL
Shadow - custom - VT
Silver Wing - tourer - GL
Spacy - scooter - CH
Sport - various - CA, CB, CE, S
Spree - scooter - NQ
Stream - three-wheeled scooter - NV
Super Cub - step thru - C
Super Dream - sports - CB
Super Hawk - sports CB
Super Sport - various - CB, CBX, SS

Transalp - trail - V, XL
Trail - C, CA, CT
Trailsport - ST
Trials - TL
Touring - CA, CD
Twinstar - custom - CM

Urban Express - moped - NU

Vision - scooter - NH

HONDA CODES

A confusing array which has built up over the years with duplications. Most are appended here, with the machine type, but without the suffix letters which usually indicated model changes.

A	first model
ATC	all terrain cycle
B	second model
C	third model
C	step-thru
C	basic series model
CA	tourer
CA	trail
CA	sports
CB	sports model
CB	custom
CB..F	sports

CB..K	sports tourer
CB..R	production racer
CBM	sports
CBR	super sports
CBX	in-line six
CBX	sports
CD	tourer
CE	sports
CF	scooter step-thru
CG	basic ohv model
CH	scooter
CJ	light sports

CL	street scrambler or trail
CM	step-thru
CM	custom
CMX	custom
CN	scooter
CP	police model
CR	racing model
CR	motocross model
CS	sports - raised exhausts
CT	trail step-thru

CT	farm bike
CX	V-twin ohv engine
CY	fun bike, balloon tyres
CYB	road racer, production based
CZ	monkey bike
D	first Dream
E	first four-stroke
EZ	trail monkey bike
F	rear wheel clip-on
FL	four-wheeled trail

FT	flat track tourer
GB	tourer
GL	farm or trail machine
GL	Gold Wing
GL	Silver Wing
H	road two-stroke
J	first Benly
K	Juno scooter
M	scooter, flat twin engine
MB	sports two-stroke
MBX	sports
ME	250cc ohc single
MF	350cc ohc single
MH	trials
MR	enduro model
MT	enduro or trail
MT	road racer
MTX	trail
NA	moped
NB	moped scooter
NC	moped
ND	moped scooter
NE	moped scooter
NF	scooter step-thru
NH	scooter
NN	moped scooter
NQ	moped scooter
NP	moped scooter
NR	New Racer
NR	eight-valve engine
NS	moped scooter
NS	sports two-stroke
NSR	works racer
NSR	sports two-stroke
NT	moped scooter
NT	road V-twin
NTV	road V-twin
NU	moped
NV	three-wheeled scooter
NX	scooter step-thru
NX	trail
P	moped, engine in rear wheel
PA	moped
PC	four-stroke moped
PC	V-four tourer
PF	moped
PM	two-stroke moped
PX	trail moped
QA	child monkey bike
QR	child motocross
RC	scrambles or street scrambler
RC	works road racer
RC	production racer
RS	road racer
RTL	trials
RVF	works racer
S	sports
SA	first 250cc ohc model
SA	moped scooter
SB	first 350cc ohc model
SB	moped scooter
SE	moped scooter
SH	moped scooter
SJ	moped scooter
SL	trail model derived from CL
SS	super sports, similar to CB
ST	miniature model, called Dax
ST	V-four tourer
TG	scooter
TL	trials model
TLM	trials moped
TLR	trials
TR	enduro
TRX	four-wheel trail
US	first ATC model
V	trail V-twin
VF	sports V-four
VFR	sports V-four
VT	sports V-twin
VTR	sports V-twin
XBR	road single
XE	enduro model with ohc engine
XL	trail model with ohc engine
XR	motocross model with ohc engine
XRV	enduro
Z	monkey bike
Z..R	motocross monkey bike

MODEL CODES BY CLASS

custom	CB, CM, CMX, CX, VT
enduro	MR, MT, TR, XE, XRV
monkey bike	CZ, EZ, QA, QR, ST, Z
moped	F, NA, NB, NC, ND, NE, NN, NQ, NP, NS, NT, NU, P, PA, PC, PF, PM, PX, SA, SH, SJ
motocross	CL, CR, MR, MT, QR, RC, XR, Z
road racing	CR, CYB, MT, RS
scooter	CF, CH, CN, K, M, NB, ND, NE, NF, NH, NN, NQ, NP, NS, NT, NV, NX, SA, SB, SE, SH, SJ, TG
sports	C, CA, CB, CBM, CBX, CS, CE, CJ, H, MB, MBX, NS, NSR, NT, S, XBR
step-thru	C, CF, CM, CT, NF, NX
super sports	CB, CBR, CBX, NR, RC, SS
tourer	C, CA, CD, CG, CS, D, FT, GL, J, ME, MF, NTV, PC, SA, SB, ST
trail	ATC, C, CA, CL, CT, CY, EZ, FL, GL, MT, MTX, NX, PX, RC, SL, ST, TRX, US, V, XL
trials	MH, RTL, TL, TLM, TLR
V-four	PC, ST, VF, VFR
V-twin	CX, NT, NTV, V, VT, VTR
works racer	NR, NSR, RC, RVF